4/9

WHY

THE
COMMON
GOOD

DO WE HAVE
TO BE ON TIME?

GRACE HOUSER

PowerKiDS
press™

New York

Published in 2019 by The Rosen Publishing Group, Inc.
29 East 21st Street, New York, NY 10010

First Edition

Editor: Jennifer Lombardo
Book Design: Tanya Dellaccio

Photo Credits: Cover Jesse Davis/Shutterstock.com; p. 5 Monkey Business Images/Shutterstock.com; p. 7 Luis Molinero/Shutterstock.com; p. 9 Anna Grigorjeva/Shutterstock.com; p. 11 martinedoucet/E+/Getty Images; p. 13 Andrey_Popov/Shutterstock.com; p. 15 XiXinXing/Shutterstock.com; p. 17 Hero Images/Getty Images; p. 19 tongcom photographer/Shutterstock.com; p. 21 RichLegg/E+/Getty Images; p. 22 razorbeam/Shutterstock.com.

Cataloging-in-Publication Data

Names: Houser, Grace.
Title: Why do we have to be on time? / Grace Houser.
Description: New York : PowerKids Press, 2019. | Series: The common good | Includes index.
Identifiers: LCCN ISBN 9781538330760 (pbk.) | ISBN 9781538330753 (library bound) | ISBN 9781538330777 (6 pack)
Subjects: LCSH: Time perception–Juvenile literature. | Self-management (Psychology)–Juvenile literature. | Children–Time management–Juvenile literature.
Classification: LCC BF468.H68 2019 | DDC 395.1′22–dc23

Manufactured in the United States of America

CPSIA Compliance Information: Batch CS18PK: For Further Information contact Rosen Publishing, New York, New York at 1-800-237-9932

CONTENTS

The Common Good

A community is a group of people who live or work in the same place. People in a community often have similar interests and values. This means they care about the same things. People can belong to many different communities. Your family is a community. Your school and classroom are also communities.

When someone does something that **benefits** their whole community, they're working toward the common good. This keeps everyone happy and keeps a community running smoothly. One way to contribute, or give, to the common good is to be on time. When you're on time, it shows that you care about others in your community.

Running Late

Think about what happens if you don't wake up when your alarm clock goes off in the morning. Your mom or dad probably yells at you to hurry up. This isn't a great way to start the day. Everyone has to rush around to get ready. It can be very **stressful**.

Sleeping in might feel good, but it can cause a lot of problems. If your parents drive you to school, they might be late to work. If you take the bus, it might have to wait for you. This makes other students late, too. Even worse, the bus might not wait at all. This is why waking up on time helps you, too.

Appointments

In a community, adults make appointments all the time. An appointment is a set time for people to do things with each other. Some people have many appointments on the same day. This makes it hard for them to change their **schedule**. To stay on schedule, everyone needs to be on time.

13

Being on time shows respect for the people you make appointments with. Running late shows you don't care about other people or their time. For example, your doctor has other **patients** to see. If you're late, then your doctor is late, which makes everyone else late. It's hard to keep a community running smoothly when this happens.

Being on Time

Being late isn't good, but neither is being too early. If you get to a party an hour before it starts, you might be in the way while people are getting ready. Be on time or only a few minutes early for important appointments and events. This will keep everyone happy and everything running on schedule.

17

Being on time doesn't always apply only to people. For example, people in a community may borrow books and movies from the local library. Borrowing means people don't need to spend money on something they might only use once or twice. However, it's important to return borrowed items on time because other people might be waiting their turn to borrow them. This shows you care for your community.

Good for Everyone

Sometimes you can't help being late. Things may happen that you can't control, such as a flat tire. If you think you might be late for an appointment, let the person you're meeting know. This shows respect and lets them **adjust** their schedule. If there are other people waiting, they might be able to take their turn before you get there.

21

When you're on time, you're working toward the common good. It shows you can be trusted and that you care about others. It also makes a good **impression** and sets a good example for others. If you're on time, you'll never have to make **excuses** for being too late or too early, and you won't mess up anyone else's plans.

GLOSSARY

adjust: To change to suit a different situation.

benefit: To be helpful or useful to.

excuse: A reason someone gives to explain something they did wrong.

impression: The effect someone or something has on a person's thoughts or feelings.

patient: A person who receives care from a doctor or nurse.

schedule: A list of times when certain events will happen.

stressful: Causing strong feelings of worry.

INDEX

WEBSITES

Due to the changing nature of Internet links, PowerKids Press has developed an online list of websites related to the subject of this book. This site is updated regularly. Please use this link to access the list: www.powerkidslinks.com/comg/time